The World's Most Advanced Sailing Education and Certification

www.nauticed.org

Navigation Rules

Authored by:

Grant Headifen
Director of Education

Cover Photo Courtesy of Beneteau

Index

What is a Hybrid eBook?

A hybrid eBook is a paper book, but when a link, animation or video is required for a fuller explanation, an App on your mobile device recognizes an associated shape and runs the appropriate multimedia presentation.

To navigate this hybrid eBook:

- First, if you have not already done so, go to www.nauticed.org and sign up for a free NauticEd Account.

- Second, download the NauticEd App from the App Store and login. Once inside the App, go to the hybrid eBook menu item. Then tap "Bring to Life" and scan this image.

Did you see the video presentation?

- Within each module of this book you will see other similar images. When you see one, scan it using the NauticEd App. It will lead you to an interactive animation, a video or a link on the Internet.

PURPOSE:

This hybrid eBook serves two purposes:

1. We believe this is one of the best basic introductions to Rules of the Nautical Road in the world. Why? Because of the ease of understanding using the

interactive animations and clear images along with the explanations.

2. This is an excellent introduction to how NauticEd sailing education works. You'll realize why interactive eLearning serves you so much better than a boring ol' paper book written in the 70's.

This course is not a required curriculum course for the NauticEd Ranks. Rather the information is already embedded into Module 5 of both the NauticEd Skipper Course and the RYA Day Skipper Course.

TEST:

You can take the test for this course for FREE to ensure you have retained the content material. Once you have created a FREE account online at NauticEd.org you will see this Navigation Rules course in your curriculum. You can take the test online or within the NauticEd App. It does not matter where you take the test, both methods report to the same database.

To gain an international sailing certification and a free Sailing Resume system from NauticEd see our online sailing certification page.

or download our FREE Sailing Certification App.

These describe the educational curriculum and the practical experience required.

NOW, please enjoy the NauticEd Navigation Rules course, you'll be a better sailor because of it.

SIDE NOTE:

We purposefully made this hybrid eBook process stupidly inexpensive despite the countless hours (and hours) of work, technology and animation expense gone into it. We did this in hopes that you would share your experience with this App and NauticEd on

and review it on the original App store. It really helps us grow - Thanks for doing that!

Because of all this, NauticEd really is the world's most advanced sailing education and certification company. We combine online and mobile App eLearning programs, an electronic sailor's logbook stored in the cloud with our worldwide network of practical sailing instructors. This creates a globally recognized real-time cloud based sailing resume that you can use to present to yacht charter companies anywhere in the world.

Our FREE sailor's electronic logbook is the most innovative in the world. With it, you can digitally authenticate your sailing experience through your crew mates. For all time, yacht charter companies have struggled believing the self stated resumes of sailors. No longer - your Authenticated NauticEd Logbook is irrefutable. Combine that with NauticEd world class eLearning education, and you can hold the most sort after Sailing Resume on the planet.

In essence, NauticEd IS the world's most advanced sailing education and sailing certification company.

View our 2 minute NauticEd entertaining video.

Now please enjoy this Navigation Rules Course.

Module 1: Introduction

Knowing the rules for safe and courteous sailing is essential for you, your family and others.

This course is a summary of the world agreed upon Navigation Rules of the nautical road known as The International Regulations for Preventing Collisions at Sea.

In saying that – note then that this is a summary AND IS NOT COMPLETE. This will however cover most of what you need to know. We do stress highly though that you actually fully read the Navigation Rules as published and agreed upon by every country in the world. The best and easiest source of this full set of rules is on the USA Coast Guard site and is at this link:

http://www.navcen.uscg.
gov/?pageName=navRulesContent

However, read our stuff here first as most is covered with explanations.

In starting, think about the enormity of this. The entire world got together and actually agreed upon something. AND even better – it is NOT some watered down document that is self-serving to special interest groups. AND even still better – it actually makes sense for everyone. AND one more even better – they are not written in legal gegal speak. Come on, all that is a HUGE WOW.

The impressive thing also about the internationally agreed upon Navigation rules is that they mostly leave out numbers and hard fast rules like for example they could have said "vessels over 50 meters shall limit their speed to 15 knots except in harbors where the speed shall not exceed 6 knots except in visibility conditions that are less that 300 meters where the speed shall be 3 knots except in the following ports ..." or something completely nautically impractical like that. What you will read and gain a real appreciation for is that in general, the document is written to hand over the duty to avoid collision to the masters of the vessels, to make sound and safe decisions based upon observation, information and experience.

It's almost like there is no big brother. That we are being trusted with our own ability to make sound decisions. That we are responsible human beings. Doesn't that give you a sense of empowerment?

But with that handover of responsibility comes the fact that we must live up to that expectation - we must know the rules. Ignorance of these rules is no excuse. Think about it like this – if you are involved in a collision, there is a 90% chance that you will be held at fault even if you were in the "right". And if you could have avoided the contact in any way, you will be held 100% responsible even if you were in the "right". How can that be you might say. Read on and you will see that the rules clearly state this.

Because you will be operating your vessel under power as well as under sail, you must learn both the rules for sailboat and the rules for power-driven vessels.

The Navigation Rules are pretty serious and so are we about this topic. On land, you could not imagine driving on the left side of the road when the local rules required you to drive on the right side. Death would come pretty quickly.

The Navigation Rules are not hard to understand or boring. So despite a desire to maybe gloss over this topic and pretend to come back to it, we want you to hunker down seriously and pay full attention here. It's THAT IMPORTANT and with our inserted discussions, we will try to keep it interesting.

By the time you reach the end of this Rules Course, we guarantee at least one thing - you will be wishing that before you go out boating next time, EVERY vessel master out there on the water has read this Course.

So straighten up your chair and pull up a Latte – let's get started. SERIOUSLY PLEASE!

(Was that a convincing enough preamble to make you want to take this seriously?)

Module 2: Introduction

Stand-On & Give-Way

We start with one vital and basic nomenclature. Worldwide, what is commonly and linguistically referred to as "Right of Way" on the land doesn't exist on the water (with the exception of "Racing Rules of Sailing"). Instead, the term "Stand-On" replaces "Right of Way".

On land, we have very strict lanes to remain in and very strict intersection rules which give rise to easily being able to determine who has the rights at any point. Now imagine 100,000 cars all going in different directions at 100 km/hr on the salt flats of Utah. Well ... let's just say it wouldn't happen for long. It would be mayhem! Thus, on the water, things are a little different. Fortunately, most of the time, the speed is less and the prudent and aware captain has time to make the proper decision according to the world recognized rules for water traffic.

The technical difference then, between Stand-On and Right of Way is that the vessel who is NOT in the Give-Way position must act predictably in the eyes of the Give-Way vessel. I.E. the Stand-On vessel is first required to maintain course and speed (Stand-On) so that the Give-Way vessel can plot a safe crossing course. If collision becomes imminent, the Stand-On vessel is then REQUIRED to take all actions possible to avoid collision. Thus, it is at this point that the Stand-On vessel technically doesn't have "rights" over the Give-Way vessel and thus the deletion of the term "Right of Way" on the water.

But what is Give-Way? It is clear inside the rules. If you

are to Give-Way, you must keep clear of the other vessel and you must not impede its ability to continue to safely operate on its passage.

So to summarize this then: in any situation, you will either be the Stand-On vessel or the Give-Way vessel. If you are the Give-Way vessel you must take visibly obvious and early actions to allow the Stand-On vessel to know that by continuing current course and speed there will be no possibility of collision. If you are the Stand-On vessel you should initially hold course and speed but it is still your final responsibility to prevent collision.

To the beginner, this new terminology has been baffling as to why the change in language for a seemingly synonymous situation. But the technical difference is valid and should be noted.

Starboard Tack - Port Tack

Only as sailors are we interested in this. It involves only the interaction between your sailboat and another sailboat. i.e. a power-driven vessel does not care where the wind is coming from and is not required to conform to any rules according to the wind. Since sailboats are driven by the wind they conform to standard navigation rules according to the wind when encountering one another.

Since the rules say a port tack boat must Give-Way to a starboard tack boat, we define those terms here. A discussion the application of the rule follows this section.

For now you must learn the definition of a starboard tack and a port tack and how to identify a boat on either.

- A sailboat is deemed to be on a port tack when the wind is coming over the port (left) side of the boat.

- A sailboat is deemed to be on a starboard tack when the wind is coming over the starboard (right) side of the boat.

When a boat is running directly downwind, you might question the above definition. The definition in the rules is clear. By its nature if a boat is on a port tack the wind of course will be pushing the sails across to the starboard side of the boat. Thus in a downwind run if the sails are on the starboard side of the boat the boat is defined as being on a port tack. Similarly, if in a downwind run if the sails are on the port side of the boat the boat is defined as being on a starboard tack.

These two boats to the left help depict that scenario where the wind is directly abaft (behind). The forward boat is on a port tack. The behind boat is on a starboard tack.

Leeward – Windward

Again, only as sailors are we interested in this. It involves only the interaction between your sailboat and another sailboat.

According to Wikipedia, the term lee derives from old English hleo, shelter, and was used as early as 900 AD. The lee side of a house was the sheltered side of the house – the downwind side. Toward the lee. Leeward! Thus on a boat, toward the lee side is the side of the boat that is furthest downwind.

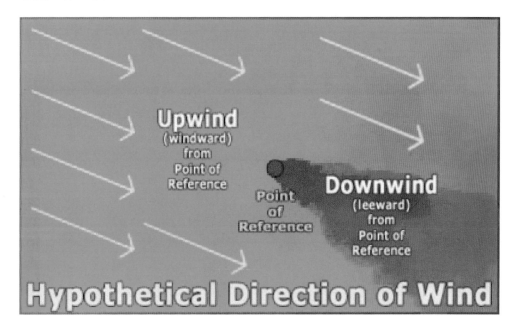

Windward then is pretty obvious. It is toward the wind. In discussing other boats, there is a reference point taken.

The reference point can be your boat, another boat, a buoy – anything. A windward boat is a boat more towards the wind than the reference point and a leeward boat is a boat more in the direction downwind of the reference point.

A leeward boat does not have to be directly downwind of another boat just that it is further downwind than the other boat.

So considering the above, you might say a boat is leeward of me. But they might be 100 meters out in front. To determine this, draw a line out in the direction of your heading, when the line gets perpendicular to the other boat, if they are then leeward of your line then they are the leeward boat at this instant (even though they might be 100 meters in out front). Here to the right, the red boat is the leeward boat.

When sailing, it is an important distinction to know if you as a sailboat are leeward or windward of another sailboat because it determines who will have to Give-Way to the other.

In general it is a given that a boat to windward is more able to maneuver than a boat to leeward because the windward boat generally has more options.

In a war, ships would gain the advantage over others by approaching them from the windward direction. And of further advantage, a leeward boat would be heeling over, presenting below the waterline planking to the windward boat. A cannon shot into this area would then more easily sink the leeward ship.

Back to modern times, we need this windward-leeward definition because further in the course you'll see the following regarding sailboats. Rule 12 of the International Regulations of Preventing Collisions at Sea stipulates that the windward sailing vessel Gives-Way to the leeward sailing vessel. This convention comes directly from the generality that the windward vessel is more maneuverable than the leeward vessel. Examples are shown in the following discussion of each rule.

Rule 3(c)- Sailboat Definition

Right now up front we're going to throw in Rule 3(c) to dispel any doubt

3(c) The term "sailing vessel" means any vessel under sail provided that propelling machinery, if fitted, is not being used.

Discussion

Rule 3(c) means that as soon as you have your engines on, even if you have you sails up, you are a power-driven vessel according to the rules.

Module 3: Seamanship

As we go through these rules we shall often state the rule and give a discussion summary thereof. Don't take the discussion as 100% gospel of the rules. The rules are the rules, our discussion is some general guidelines to help (there - we just covered ourselves legally).

Rule 2: Responsibility

The Rule

a. *Nothing in these Rules shall exonerate any vessel, or the owner, master, or crew thereof, from the consequences of any neglect to comply with these Rules or of the neglect of any precaution which may be required by the ordinary practice of seamen, or by the special circumstances of the case.*

b. *In construing and complying with these Rules due regard shall be had to all dangers of navigation and collision and to any special circumstances, including the limitations of the vessels involved, which may make a departure from these Rules necessary to avoid immediate danger.*

Discussion

The rules refer many times to good seamanship. This is a good catch all so that a judge can make a decision around "Was the vessel master who appeared to have Stand-On rights, still acting with common sense?". This question means a decision can go anyway and will probably eventually be argued out in reality with the side that pays the most money to a team of lawyers. As bad and poor a statement about society as that is – it is just reality – get over it. In an idealistic world, the Judges would filter out the $ and make a sound decision, but that is not necessarily reality either.

Good seamanship comes from experience and it is for this reason that operating as the master of large commercial ships require years of experience. BUT the same seamanship rule is applied all the way down to a kayak because Rule 1(a) says these rules apply to all vessels.

Operating without good seamanship even though you were the Stand-On vessel could result in you being liable for the accident. As you read through the rules below it will become apparent that perhaps this is surprisingly and unexpected fair statement.

The best advice we can give here around seamanship is to get experience. If you have never been on a boat before, it's probably not a good idea to buy one outright and operate as the master. Gain lots of crewing experience. If you're just getting started in sailing, go join your local yacht club and crew in regattas. This will be your fastest learning curve.

Module 4: Sailboats v. Sailboats

Sailboats On The Same Tack

Rule 12 (a)

(ii) when both have the wind on the same side, the vessel which is to windward shall keep out of the way of the vessel which is to leeward;

Examples

Several Scenarios are presented below as same tack Give-Way examples:

This video shows a windward boat approaching from the upper left of the screen whilst the leeward boat is approaching from the bottom left. Both sailboats are on port tacks. The windward boat correctly alters course to duck in behind the leeward boat.

Now can you figure out this scenario?

The boat you are standing on is on port tack because you can see the headsail is being blown to the starboard side of the boat. The boat approaching is also on a port tack since you can also see that their headsail is on their starboard side. Under this scenario you are furthermost downwind and the leeward boat. Therefore, they must Give-Way. Caution however, their sails may be blocking their view of you and therefore, it is prudent to hail "LEEWARD".

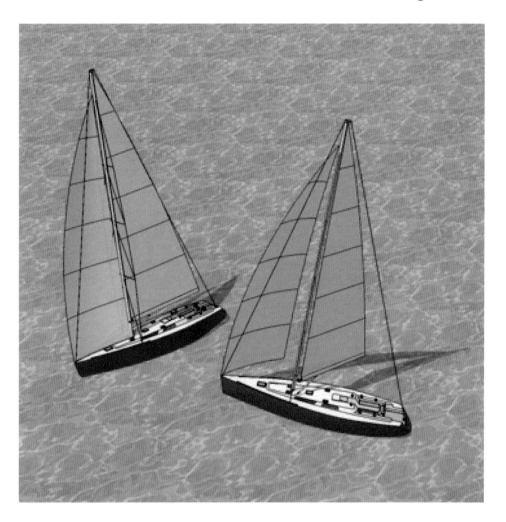

Above: From the set of the sails, the wind is obviously from bottom to top on the image. Therefore, Blue is on Port, Red is also on Port. Red is the leeward boat and therefore is the stand-on vessel. Thus, Blue must Give-Way and in a hurry from the looks of it. The best action here would be for Blue to steer up into the wind - turn to port - NOW! However, every circumstance is different and a "judgment call". The reason we'd recommend an immediate turn to port for Blue is because it would be turning away from Red. Trying to duck (going behind) is risky because you are turning towards Red and depending on your speed you could hit Red. A turn to port will allow Red to give room without any risk of collision.

Above: Again from the set of the sails, the wind is coming from the bottom left to the top right on the image and Red and Blue are both on Port. Red is the leeward boat. Blue must Give-Way. The best course of action would probably be to turn upwind and tighten sails, although a gybe would work as well depending on Blue's desired course and taking into account that in high winds, gybes are dangerous for the crew and for the rig.

Sailboats on Opposite Tacks

Rule 12(a)

(i) when each has the wind on a different side, the vessel which has the wind on the port side shall keep out of the way of the other

Discussion

In olden times the steerboard (rudder) was mounted typically on the right side of the boat. In order to prevent damage to the steerboard a boat would dock it's left side to the dock (port). Thus via language, accents and time boats sides became referred to as starboard and port. When a boat was sailing with the wind coming first over its right side the boat is said to be on a starboard tack. It thus heels to port. With the heeling effect this meant that a boat with its rudder mounted to the starboard side of the boat it would have less of its rudder in the water. This would make the boat less maneuverable than boats on the opposite tack who had their full rudder length in the water. And so became the convention of port tack (more maneuverable) boats must Give-Way to starboard tack (less maneuverable) boats. Now virtually all boats have their rudder in the center. However, the convention has held steadfast.

At all times you must know what tack you are on and constantly be assessing what tack other boats around you are on. The rule also states that if a vessel with the wind on the port side sees a vessel to windward and cannot determine with certainty whether the other vessel has the wind on the port or on the starboard side, she shall keep out of the way of the other.

Examples

In the video below, you can see several examples of two sailboats on a collision course. The sailboat on a port tack correctly changes course or tacks away to avoid the sailboat on a starboard tack. The decision to tack or change course to "duck" behind the aft of the starboard vessel is up to you. The video refers to Rule 10 which is under ISAF rules of racing which is exactly the same as this International Rule 12.

Here are two more static examples:

Above: From the set of the sails the wind is from bottom right to top left on the image. Therefore, Red is on Starboard (wind blowing sail to port), Blue is on Port (wind blowing headsail to starboard). Thus, Blue must Give-Way. Blue could release sails and turn down wind or tack. Either action had better be NOW! We'd estimate here that Blue is better off letting sails out and bearing away from the wind to pass behind Red. It is probably too late to tack because of the forward momentum of the vessel. Also of note, if Red was to take evasive maneuvers to avoid Blue, Red should tack, turning to starboard. IE evasive maneuvers should always be in the direction away from the vessel and in a direction that would not cause a collision should the other vessel make last second maneuvers. In this example, if Red turns to starboard, the chance of collision would be significantly reduced.

Above: From the set of the sails the wind must be blowing from top left to bottom right on the image. Therefore, Blue is "on starboard" and Red is "on port". Red must Give-Way. The best course of action would probably be for Red to turn further downwind to starboard - perhaps even causing a gybe.

Unsure

Especially at night, but also many times when viewing a sailing vessel you might be unsure about its tack. Well the rules cover this also.

Rule 12(a)

(iii) if a vessel with the wind on the port side sees a vessel to windward and cannot determine with certainty whether the other vessel has the wind on the port or on the starboard side, she shall keep out of the way of the other.

Running

The Rules also cover running directly downwind where the wind is directly abaft and not coming over either side of the sailboat.

Rule 12(b)

For the purposes of this Rule the windward side shall be deemed to be the side opposite that on which the mainsail is carried or, in the case of a square-rigged vessel, the side opposite to that on which the largest fore-and-aft sail is carried.

Discussion

The two boats below are Running. The forward boat is on port. The rear boat is on starboard.

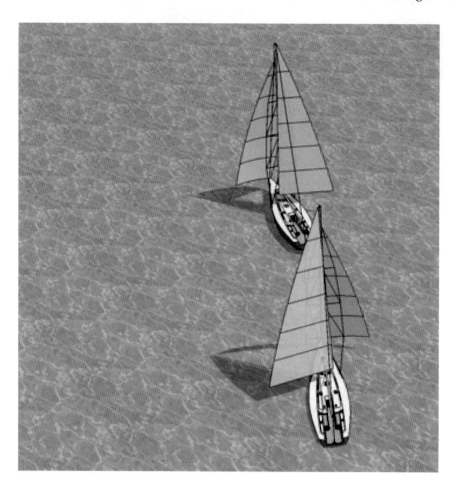

One Sailboat Overtaking Another

When one sailboat is overtaking another sailboat we refer you to the next module which discusses Rule 13 overtaking. This overtaking rule seems like it could be a contradiction, in certain circumstances but it is not. Rule 13 is the overriding rule, it takes precedence over the other rules.

For example, when a sailboat on starboard is overtaking a sailboat on port - it is the starboard sailboat that must Give-Way not the port sailboat. See the next module for examples and discussion.

Module 5: Sailboats v Powerboats

Rule 3(c)

The term "sailing vessel" means any vessel under sail provided that propelling machinery, if fitted, is not being used.

Discussion

A Sailboat Under Engine Power is a Power-Driven Vessel. Also note "being used" - your lawyer might argue that "being used" means that the engine was being used to propel. The other side's lawyer would argue that "being used" was "on". I doubt if you want to get into the expense of that argument. Assume that if you are a sailboat and your engine is on you are a powerboat. It means you can't be a smarty pants and slip your gear into neutral before a collision and argue that your engine was not being used. Nor can you switch off your engine and argue that your engine was not being used. Even your insurance company would look at you strange and would pay up - they don't want the expense of that battle either.

So what about this, you're under sail with engines off and in an immanent collision situation with a powerboat. If you turn your engines on you could avoid the collision. What do you do? The answer lies in "What would a good seaman do to avoid collision?"

Examples

Above: The sailboat must Give-Way to the powerboat because (1) The sailboat is now a powerboat and (2) the powerboat is on the starboard side of the sailboat.

Above: The sailboat is the Stand-On vessel because both vessels are considered powerboats and the powerboat is on the port side of the sailboat.

 Above: Scan to play the video. The two sailboats have their engines on. They are now both classified as power driven vessels. The sailboat which has the other sailboat on their starboard must Give-Way.

Remember this by imagining what color light would you see on the other boat. If you see red, like in a traffic light you must give-way. Using the mnemonic "Is there any red port left", the red light is on the port side of the boat.

Module 6: Overtaking

Here we quote the rules exactly because they are incredibly clear. Note that a sailing vessel is part of "any vessel". i.e. if you are a sailing vessel overtaking any other vessel according to (a) you must keep clear.

Rule 13

a. *Notwithstanding anything contained in the Rules, any vessel overtaking any other shall keep out of the way of the vessel being overtaken.*

b. *A vessel shall be deemed to be overtaking when coming up with a another vessel from a direction more than 22.5 degrees abaft her beam*

c. *When a vessel is in any doubt as to whether she is overtaking another, she shall assume that this is the case and act accordingly.*

d. *Any subsequent alteration of the bearing between the two vessels shall not make the overtaking vessel a crossing vessel within the meaning of these Rules or relieve her of the duty of keeping clear of the overtaken vessel until she is finally past and clear.*

Discussion

Wow look at (d). This means that even while you are overtaking and keeping clear, if the other vessel changes course you must still keep clear. But there is nothing in (d) that says if you are being overtaken that you have the right to change course. If you are being overtaken you are obligated to continue to Stand-On to not make course changes.

Do you get the overall feeling here? There is a common theme. The rules are written so that everyone has the responsibility to avoid collision. Even if you feel you are in the right – you can not instigate a collision to prove your point.

Some Examples

Above: The sailboat is overtaking a powerboat. Any vessel overtaking another must Give-Way, therefore the sailboat must Give-Way. This is also the case if the powerboat was lying adrift in this position.

However, if the powerboat was adrift in the position in the

image below, the powerboat must Give-Way. The reason for this is that adrift is actually considered as "underway" even with engines off. Often times in lakes or sheltered bays we will encounter powerboats that are adrift as such sunbathing etc. The rules are clear - adrift is underway and appropriate Giving Way must be done. However, the rules are also clear in that you must avoid collision. Therefore, if you determine that the skipper of a powerboat that is adrift is not getting up and shifting out of your way then you must avoid the adrift powerboat AND you must do so in order to not create a close quarters situation. In any case this is one of those situations where a little courtesy should also be applied. The choice now becomes, which way should you go, windward or leeward of the vessel? Going windward in a close hauled sail set could be dangerous because your vessel always has a certain amount of side-slip and you just might not make it - or the wind could change, causing you not to be able to make as tight of a heading as you estimated. Going in front of the boat also has it's concerns, because if the captain suddenly turned on engines in a panic to get out of your way he might steer right into you. In this situation, if the boat were not taking evasive maneuvers, we'd recommend loudly announcing your intentions preferably with a whistle or horn, bearing away from the wind and pass well clear to the lee (downwind) of the vessel.

Above: the adrift powerboat must Give-Way to the sailboat.

Above: Is an interesting one. The trailing sailboat on is on starboard and the leading sailboat is on port. Which do you think must Give-Way? Well for a collision to exist, the rear must be overtaking the leader. The overtaking vessel must Give-Way even though she is on starboard. In this case starboard Gives-Way to port. Don't get confused, just remember that an overtaking boat Gives-Way to the other. Which is a pretty obvious logical rule and as you'll see later - being Overtaken is at the top of the pecking order of Stand-On.

Module 7: Lookout

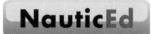

Rule 5

Every vessel shall at all times maintain a proper look-out by sight and hearing as well as by all available means appropriate in the prevailing circumstances and conditions so as to make a full appraisal of the situation and of the risk of collision.

Discussion

This is pretty clear. It means that if you have a collision because you did not see the other vessel (even if you were the Stand-On vessel) you can be deemed to be at fault because you failed this rule.

This is particularly possible in a sailboat situation because of the headsail tending to block almost 60 degrees of your visibility to the leeward side of the boat.

Thus for example, if you are a sailboat on a starboard tack, you know you are the Stand-On boat over port tack sailboats. However, you still have the responsibility to maintain a proper lookout in your blind spot. If you fail this you could be held at least partially at fault.

The last thing you want to see looking under the headsail is this:

This sailboat is on a port tack. BUT you should have seen this coming before immanent collision.

Are you getting all this? You may think you have rights and are stand-on, BUT you have responsibilities operating a vessel. Keep this in mind as you go through the remainder of the course. There is no place on the water (or the court room)for ego, stubbornness and righteousness.

Read our real story of a near collision due to failure to keep a look-out i.e. asleep at the helm! (Links to our online sailing blog site)

Module 8: Safe Speed

Rule 6

Every vessel shall at all times proceed at a safe speed so that she can take proper and effective action to avoid collision and be stopped within a distance appropriate to the prevailing circumstances and conditions.

In determining a safe speed the following factors shall be among those taken into account:

a. *By all vessels:*

    i. *The state of visibility;*

    ii. *The traffic density including concentrations of fishing vessels or any other vessels;*

    iii. *The manageability of the vessel with special reference to stopping distance and turning ability in the prevailing conditions;*

    iv. *At night, the presence of background light such as from shore lights or from back scatter from her own lights;*

    v. *The state of wind, sea and current, and the proximity of navigational hazards;*

    vi. *The draft in relation to the available depth of water.*

b. *Additionally, by vessels with operational radar:*

    i. *The characteristics, efficiency and limitations of the radar equipment;*

    ii. *Any constraints imposed by the radar range*

scale in use;

iii. *The effect on radar detection of the sea state, weather and other sources of interference;*

iv. *The possibility that small vessels, ice and other floating objects may not be detected by radar at an adequate range;*

v. *The number, location and movement of vessels detected by radar;*

vi. *The more exact assessment of the visibility that may be possible when radar is used to determine the range of vessels or other objects in the vicinity.*

Discussion

This rule is another good example of leaving the responsibility to good seamanship. You can see that it was also written without any legal-gegal. Just plain and simple. And even without being a good seaman (person), anyone can see that these are common sense rules.

Module 9: Risk of Collision

Rule 7

a. *Every vessel shall use all available means appropriate to the prevailing circumstances and conditions to determine if risk of collision exists. If there is any doubt such risk shall be deemed to exist.*

b. *Proper use shall be made of radar equipment if fitted and operational, including long-range scanning to obtain early warning of risk of collision and radar plotting or equivalent systematic observation of detected objects.*

c. *Assumptions shall not be made on the basis of scanty information, especially scanty radar information.*

d. *In determining if risk of collision exists the following considerations shall be among those taken into account:*

   i. *Such risk shall be deemed to exist if the compass bearing of an approaching vessel does not appreciably change.*

   ii. *Such risk may sometimes exist even when an appreciable bearing change is evident, particularly when approaching a very large vessel or a tow or when approaching a vessel at close range.*

Discussion

Here it is saying that you are fully responsible for determining if any risk exists and that you MUST use all available means to determine the risk. Part (c) says that you can't make assumptions on scanty information i.e. you must be fully confident that the information you are receiving is 100% reliable.

Take an example of you failing to take the action of determining risk and a collision happened but fortunately you were not the Give-Way vessel. This rule says that you are accountable for the collision.

Below we show what it means by a constant compass bearing of an approaching vessel. Scan the image code for the animation.

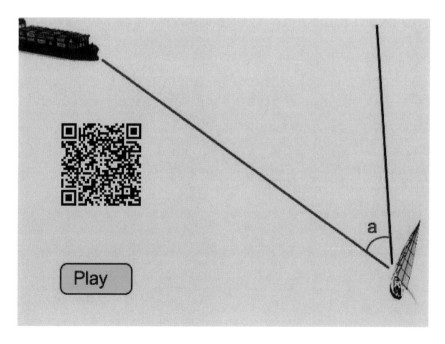

A compass bearing is more reliable than lining two points

up on your boat because if the heading of your boat changes the line will change. Using a compass bearing - the bearing does not care if your heading changes. The bearing will remain the same.

This is also a good time to introduce you to AIS

In the United States and most other countries, all commercial traffic with gross tonnage above 300 tons and all passenger vessels are required to transmit AIS Data. AIS uses a digital VHF signal and stands for Automatic Identification System. With AIS you can get data on shipping traffic, the name of the vessel, the heading, speed, the GPS position and other data. A good example of a real-time site showing AIS data is http://www.shipais.com. The image below is from this website and is of the Solent area in the south of the UK. You can hover over a ship with your mouse and get the information, which can help avoid collisions. Wikipedia has a good explanation of AIS.

Also watch this AIS video done by NauticEd's friend, Chuck Hawley formerly of West Marine HQ. Chuck does a really great explanation of the AIS technology.

Plot of Traffic in the UK

www.shipais.com

This is an image capture of AIS traffic in the Solent, UK. When you scan the image code you can see traffic in real time. You will get heading, speed, destination, vessel name, vessel size information.

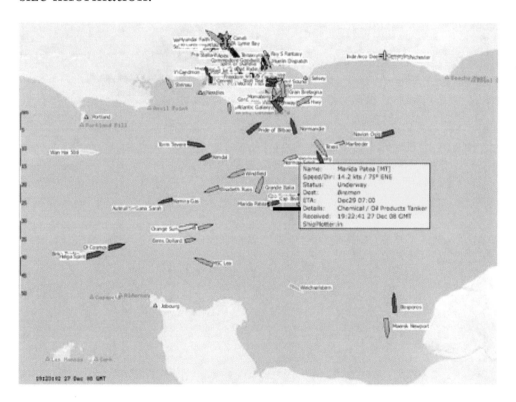

Plot of Traffic in the USA

www.marinetraffic.com

Below is an image capture of San Francisco Bay.

Module 10: Action to Avoid Collision

When you reach the section on who is responsible to Give-Way to who you'll see that in certain circumstances a large container ship must Give-Way to a sailboat. Hmmmm - let's think about this one before we go enforcing our "rights".

If you saw this above now who should Give-Way? This rule here is all about avoiding a collision and will clearly put you at fault if you fail to take action.

Rule 8

a. *Any action shall [be taken in accordance with the Rules of this Part and], if the circumstances of the case admit, be positive, made in ample time and with due regard to the observance of good seamanship.*

b. *Any alteration of course and/or speed to avoid*

collision shall, if the circumstances of the case admit, be large enough to be readily apparent to another vessel observing visually or by radar; a succession of small alterations of course and/or speed should be avoided.

c.   If there is sufficient sea room, alteration of course alone may be the most effective action to avoid a close-quarters situation provided that it is made in good time, is substantial and does not result in another close-quarters situation.

d.   Action taken to avoid collision with another vessel shall be such as to result in passing at a safe distance. The effectiveness of the action shall be carefully checked until the other vessel is finally past and clear.

e.   If necessary to avoid collision or allow more time to assess the situation, a vessel may slacken her speed or take all way off by stopping or reversing her means of propulsion.

f.

   i.   A vessel which, by any of these rules, is required not to impede the passage or safe passage of another vessel shall, when required by the circumstances of the case, take early action to allow sufficient sea room for the safe passage of the other vessel.

   ii. A vessel required not to impede the passage or safe passage of another vessel is not relieved of this obligation if approaching the other vessel so as to involve risk of collision and shall, when taking action, have full regard to the action which may be required by the rules of this part.

   iii. A vessel, the passage of which is not to be impeded remains fully obliged to comply with the rules of this part when the two vessels are approaching one another so as to involve risk of collision.

Discussion

Parts (a) through (e) do not refer solely to the Give-Way vessel. It is taking about any action. In particular parts (c) and (d) should be of EXTREME NOTICE. They say you should avoid a close quarters situation and pass at a safe distance. For example, if there is any doubt as to whether you could cut in front of another vessel and it might get a wee bit close, the rule says you can not.

Anecdote:

One time in my younger days I was out windsurfing. There was a large party barge crossing the path were all the windsurfers were cutting back and forth. To myself I said "I am driven by wind. I have the right of way" and so I proceeded to cut in front believing I had enough room to make it and besides he had to get out of my way. As I crossed in front, he was so large that he stole my wind and I ended up in the drink RIGHT IN FRONT OF A PARTY BARGE with my harness still hooked in. That could have been the death of me because I was enforcing my rights. However, a quick look at 8(c) would have ended up with my relatives paying to clean the blood off the prop. I created a close quarters situation.

Rules 8(c) and (d) prevent you from getting close. Don't get close. Anyways choose the safe route.

At this stage you might be getting what we are talking about

BUT have some dilemma trying to balance Stand-On and choosing safe. The Rules are still clear on this – it talks about early action – the Stand-On vessel MAY take early action:

- communication – early and substantial course change,

- no close quarters situation - staying a safe distance apart,

- acting according to full knowledge not scanty knowledge,

- good seamanship

Module 11: Interactions With Large Traffic

Rules 9 and 10 deal with Narrow channels and Traffic separation schemes and mainly refer to larger commercial traffic, but there are some gems you need to know as a sailboat because you are in essence interacting with the other traffic.

In a traffic separation scheme, traffic Lanes are set aside for the safe operation of traffic in high density areas. Much like a highway, traffic flows in singular directions in each lane and there is a separation zone between them. Unlike highways there are no painted lines or necessarily any signs. Rather, they are shown on charts. You must be cognizant of the locations of these lanes and any route planning should pre-identify these lanes.

Narrow channels are more obvious. They are usually the entrance to a harbor or a river or inland waterway or dredged channel. They are often marked by the shore or by channel markers.

Here are a few gems on thought:

- Gem (1) When proceeding along a narrow channel, keep the edge of the channel as close to your starboard side as safe and practically possible. This makes it difficult to prudently and safely sail when in a narrow channel. i.e. play it safe turn on engines a and pull the sails down. This is not an ego contest.

- Gem (2) As a sailboat under power or sail, you can not impede the passage of a vessel which can safely navigate only within a narrow channel of fairway.

- Gem (3) No anchoring in a narrow channel or traffic

lanes or even traffic separation zones.

- Gem (4) If you must cross a traffic separation lane, cross at right angles.

- Gem (5) A vessel of less than 20 meters in length or a sailing vessel shall not impede the safe passage of a power-driven vessel following a traffic lane. i.e. Give-Way to all power vessels in a traffic lane. Yes as a sailboat (less than 20 m), you must even Give-Way to a large recreational motor launch for example.

Advice: Stay out of traffic schemes as much as possible.

Module 12: Head-On Situations

Rule 14

(a) *Unless otherwise agreed when two power-driven vessels are meeting on reciprocal or nearly reciprocal courses so as to involve risk of collision each shall alter her course to starboard so that each shall pass on the port side of the other.*

(c) *When a vessel is in any doubt as to whether such a situation exists she shall assume that it does exist and act accordingly.*

Discussion

The agreement above can be established via VHF, light or sound signals.

When two sailboats are approaching head on the rule of opposite tacks is in effect.

Typically, vessels in a head on situation will each turn to starboard. The audible announcement of this is 1 one second blast.

  Short

Tap the image when it loads on your device.

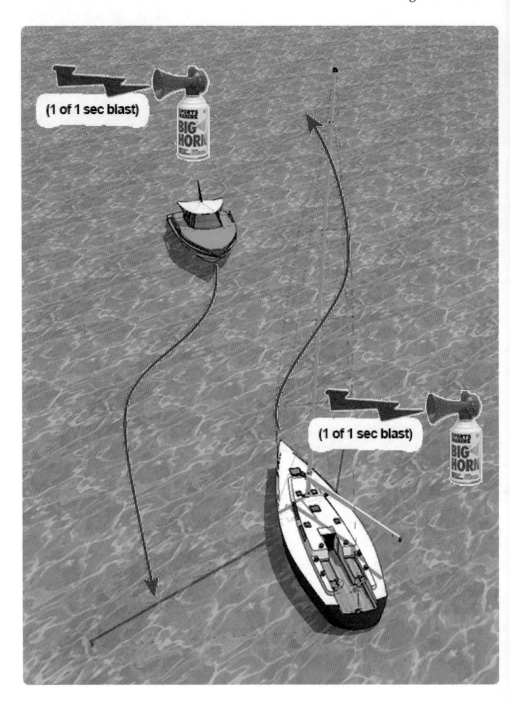

Module 13: Crossing Situations

Rule 15

15 (a) When two power-driven vessels are crossing so as to involve risk of collision, the vessel which has the other on her own starboard side shall keep out of the way and shall, if the circumstances of the case admit, avoid crossing ahead of the other vessel.

Discussion

There is an easy way to remember this.

First repeat this mantra to yourself which for most of us is easy to remember referring to red port wine.

"Is there any RED PORT LEFT?"

It means that the left side of your boat is the port side and the light color on it is red.

Knowing that red lights on boats are positioned on the port side of the vessel and green lights are positioned on the starboard side of the vessel, an easy way to remember this crossing rule is that the vessel required per this rule to stay clear of the other will see the red light side of the other vessel. In our normal everyday driving situations a red light means stop and a green light means go. Thus, the vessel seeing the green light side of the other vessel is the Stand-On vessel. The vessel seeing the red light is the Give-Way vessel.

Note this says power-driven vessels so it does not apply to sailboats under sail with engines off. And also note – you can't try to be tricky and turn your engines off. The rule says

"… as to involve the risk of collision". You entered the involving situation under power so the power-driven rule applies to you at the onset.

In this case the sailboat is a power-driven vessel. It is in a crossing situation with another power-driven vessel. The sailboat will see the red light side of the powerboat and so here the sailboat must keep clear of the power boat and it should avoid crossing in front of the powerboat. And in such a turn it should not turn towards the powerboat. Thus, the only real action left to avoid collision and keep clear is for the sailboat to turn hard to port.

Module 14: Action by Give-Way Vessels

Rule 16

Every vessel which is directed to keep out of the way of another vessel shall, so far as possible, take early and substantial action to keep well clear.

Discussion

This rule was designed well. It means that for example if you are the Give-Way vessel that you are communicating (via the action of your vessel) to the other vessel that you have seen them and are taking the appropriate action. Without this clear communication, you are leaving the other vessel guessing as to whether you have seen them or not.

Imagine you are a Stand-On vessel. Any other another vessel on a possible collision course should make you pretty nervous. However, if they communicate to you that they have seen you then your stress level is going to be reduced. The early and substantial action to keep well clear is exactly that communication. Substantial action is best done as a major course change. Rule 8(b) even says that a succession of small alterations of course and/or speed should be avoided.

Communication of knowledge of the situation however is the key. Even in a sailboat racing situation where substantial action is typically not given, the helms-person of the Give-Way vessel should communicate to the other that they have seen them via verbal acknowledgment and a wave signal.

The rule also says well clear. It does not say by 1, 2, 5 , 10 meters. It says well clear. How clear is well clear? Clear enough using good seamanship - that's how well clear.

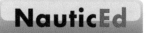

Module 15: Action by Stand-On Vessels

Strangely enough, the written text for action of a Stand-On vessel is longer than that of a Give-Way vessel.

Rule 17 (a)

(a) (i) Where one of two vessels is to keep out of the way, the other shall keep her course and speed.

(ii) The latter vessel may however take action to avoid collision by her maneuver alone, as soon as it becomes apparent to her that the vessel required to keep out of the way is not taking appropriate action in compliance with these Rules.

Discussion

Maintaining course and speed is also communicating to the Give-Way vessel and setting a predictable path whereby the Give-Way vessel can take appropriate actions. Predictability is the crux of "Stand-On". Ever played dance with someone in the grocery store? You're on a head on collision in the pastry section, she moves right at the same time you move left. Next thing you know you're crashing into each other. It's ok in the grocery store and you might even get a date out of it – on the seas the only date will be one in court.

Note that the rule also says that the Stand-On vessel MAY take action to avoid collision as soon as it becomes apparent that the Give-Way vessel is not taking the appropriate action.

Rule 17 (b)

(b) When, from any cause, the vessel required to keep her

course and speed finds herself so close that collision cannot be avoided by the action of the Give-Way vessel alone, she shall take such action as will best aid to avoid collision.

Discussion

For such a small subsection, this rule is one of the most important rules of all. It says that the Stand-On vessel SHALL take action to avoid collision. It totally takes away your rights in court to argue that you were the Stand-On vessel. If it is deemed that you knew or should have known about the other vessel and did not take action to avoid the collision YOU are the one at fault.

Anecdote

Read this blog article I wrote which shows a major life threatening situation I was in where I was the Stand-On vessel (I was anchored) yet had the collision occurred, I could have been held responsible.

http://www.nauticed.org/sailing-blog/mayday-may-day-mayday-collision-at-sea/

Module 16: Responsibility Between Vessels

Every vessel has a definition of being one and only one of the below at all times. And each vessel has the ability to morph from one to the other. A fishing vessel may haul in its nets. A sailboat may turn on its engines. A container ship may move from the open ocean into a narrow channel.

Thus, you have the responsibility of determining what is the vessel definition whereby you have a collision potential and you will take actions accordingly and know what status you have - Stand-On or Give-Way.

Rule 18

Here is a summary discussion of Rule 18

OVERTAKEN: Vessels being overtaken are the Stand-on vessel. No matter what type you are, if you are overtaking another vessel, you must Give-Way to that vessel.

NOT UNDER COMMAND: This means vessels that may somehow be disabled due to extraordinary circumstances such as mechanical means or if the crew is out of action. This is certainly a very unusual case and not very likely to happen but the rules put this case at the top of the order of Stand-On vessels. I.E. It means that if a boat is moving or drifting and not able to control itself then you should Give Way to it. Durh!

RESTRICTED IN ITS ABILITY TO MANEUVER: This usually refers to large commercial vessels in shipping lanes, barges, or vessels engaged in towing, drilling or dredging. Well durh again - of course this makes sense.

CONSTRAINED BY DRAFT: This refers to vessels that are in channels, rivers etc and causing them to maneuver out of your way would possibly cause them to run aground. Durh of course!

FISHING VESSELS ENGAGED IN FISHING: The term "vessel engaged in fishing" means any vessel fishing with nets, lines, trawls, or other fishing apparatus which restrict maneuverability, but does not include a vessel fishing with trolling lines or other fishing apparatus which do not restrict manageability.

(Note as a fisherman AND a sailor – I employ a little courtesy here as well i.e. if someone is trolling, why not tack away early with a smile and a wave?)

SAILING VESSELS UNDERWAY: The term "sailing vessel" means any vessel under sail provided that propelling machinery, if fitted, is not being used.

POWER-DRIVEN VESSELS: The term 'power-driven vessel' means any vessel propelled by machinery. i.e. These are power driven vessels that do not fall into any of the categories above.

SEAPLANES: Strange one - but they have to come somewhere. Now of course a plane that is making an emergency water landing is classified as a Vessel not under command. Better get out of its way!

WIG CRAFT: This is a relatively new category. They are essentially seaplanes but fly near the surface of the water using lift from the ground effect phenomenon.

The above is the internationally recognized pecking order of who is the Stand-On vessel over the vessel below it. e.g. fishing vessels engaged in fishing as defined above are the Stand-On vessel over sailboats.

Please memory erase the ill-informed statement made by anyone at the yacht club that sailboats have the right of way over everyone else. THEY ARE WRONG.

The pecking order of who is to Give-Way to who is logically defined from a vessel's ability to get out of the way of another. And since sailboats are quite maneuverable they are actually quite a way down the pecking order of who is the Stand-On vessel.

The Mnemonic that most people use to remember the order is this:

Only New Reels Catch Fish So Purchase Some.

- **O**vertaken
- **N**ot Under Command
- **R**estricted in Maneuverability
- **C**onstrained by Draft
- **F**ishing
- **S**ailing
- **P**ower
- **S**eaplanes

Module 17: Vessels In Restricted Visibility

Rule 19

a. *This Rule applies to vessels not in sight of one another when navigating in or near an area of restricted visibility.*

b. *Every vessel shall proceed at a safe speed adapted to the prevailing circumstances and conditions of restricted visibility. A power-driven vessel shall have her engines ready for immediate maneuver.*

c. *Every vessel shall have due regard to the prevailing circumstances and conditions of restricted visibility when complying with the Rules [of Section I of this Part | 4 through 10].*

d. *A vessel which detects by radar alone the presence of another vessel shall determine if a close-quarters situation is developing [and/or | or] or risk of collision exists. If so, she shall take avoiding action in ample time, provided that when such action consists of an alteration in course, so far as possible the following shall be AVOIDED:*

   i. *An alteration of course to port for a vessel forward of the beam, other than for a vessel being overtaken;*

   ii. *An alteration of course toward a vessel abeam or abaft the beam.*

e. *Except where it has been determined that a risk of collision does not exist, every vessel which hears apparently forward of her beam the fog signal of another vessel, or which cannot avoid a close-quarters situation with another vessel forward of her beam, shall reduce her speed to be the minimum at which she can be kept on her course. She shall if*

*necessary take all her way off and in any event navigate
with extreme caution until danger of collision is over.*

Discussion

What is the safe speed at night, in fog? As safe as it needs
to be under good seamanship.

Module 18: A Review So Far

We hope you have gained a real appreciation for our outlook so far on the rules. Our biggest point to stress is that even if you think you have rights - you can't force them according to the rules. They make that very clear. You have to stay a safe distance away.

The basic sailboat "Rules of the Road" (on the water) are:

- You must act to avoid a collision even if you are the Stand-On vessel.

- A sailboat on port tack must Give Way to a sailboat on starboard tack.

- If two sailboats are on the same tack, the leeward (furthermost downwind) sailboat is the Stand-On vessel.

- When under power and meeting head on, both boats turn to starboard and pass port to port were possible.

- If a sailboat is overtaking a power-driven vessel then the sailboat must Give Way

- When a sailboat is using its engine then it is automatically classified as a power-driven vessel and loses all rights as a sailboat.

- When a sailboat is using its engine, it must Give Way to other power-driven vessels approaching from its starboard side.

- You may deviate from any rule in order to avoid immediate danger.

- Learn the "Pecking Order" of who gives way to who.

There are more rules - read the full rules at

http://www.navcen.uscg.gov/?pageName=navRulesContent

Now look at the Rules regarding lights starting in the next module.

Module 19: Lights and Shapes

Introduction

Night time can be a beautiful time to sail. However, night vision is not the same as day vision and so rules have been established to ensure safety. Regardless of visibility, due to nighttime, fog or cloudy conditions, garish distracting city lights, or clear romantic moonlit skies, sailors need to know their colors, lighting requirements and shapes.

Powerboats, large shipping vessels and vessels at anchor will display a variety of lights, some steady and some flashing at regular intervals. All of these are providing essential information to help avoid collisions. Navigation lights are not meant to entertain, or emulate Christmas trees.

Night Sailing Requirements (and day shapes)

Your responsibility, when sailing in diminished lighting conditions and after sunset and before sunrise is to turn your navigation lights on. Don't assume they are working - the sea salt environment is a poor environment to expect electrical contact to continuously work. Visually check for operation after you turn them on.

All vessel types have a unique distinguishing set of lights that they must adhere to depending on the type of vessel. i.e. Sailing, towing, fishing, restricted in ability to maneuver, constrained by draft, dredging, etc. It would be prudent for you to learn all the differences in these lights - hint some are on the test. However, there are Apps, lookup charts and tools that you can stow on board so that you don't have to rely on 100% functionality of your brain cells.

Reference Tools

A good tool by Weems and Plath is the light slide rule available at:

http://www.landfallnavigation.com/lightroadrule.html.

You simply slide the card in its sleeve until you see the matching set of lights to your observed vessel.

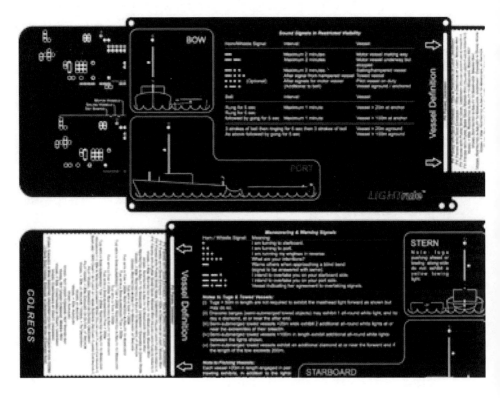

Having said this, there are also good Apps available.

Apps

In the following section of this eBook, we show the light requirements but you might not always have your tablet device with you. Chances are you will have your phone with you and there are good phone Apps available. You should download one now - you never know when you will need it.

Here are three available for iOS

ColRegs: Nav Lights & Shapes for Boating and Sailing

Lights and Shapes COLREG

Lights and shapes - Sergio Guaita

On The Web

The lights for all vessels are covered in the Navigation Rules printed by the USGC and apply to international rules as well. They are Part C Rules 20 through 31.

You can get the latest version in book format on your Kindle or using the Kindle App.

The Rules for Vessels

For sailing vessels the lights required internationally are:

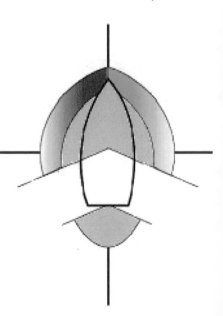

- Bow or top of mast – red (port side) and green (starboard side) with a 112.5 degrees arc - remember "is there any red port left"

- Mast head - white (360 degrees for anchored only)

- Mast head - white (225 degrees facing forward for under power only)

- Stern - white with a 135 degrees arc

- Optional - Masthead 360 degrees red over green

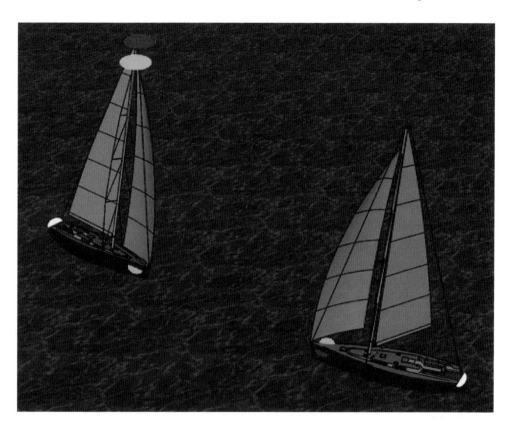

When sailing at night and meeting another vessel (that you do not want to hit) remember that your starboard light is green and your port light is red. The same as the lights of the oncoming vessel.

When meeting head on, the color light on your vessel will pass the approaching vessel's same color light. For example, if you are passing starboard to starboard (the starboard side of your vessel will see the starboard side of the other vessel) your green light will meet the green light on the other vessel. Or you may pass port to port (red light to red light). If you see red and green on the other vessel, they are heading directly at you. When in a head-on situation, and you are the Stand On vessel, it is at your discretion as to whether you pass port to port or starboard to starboard and the decision will be dependent upon the conditions. When in a head-on situation, powerboats typically pass port to port. Thus it is prudent that a sailboat to do the same if practical. Make your turn large and obvious for the other boat to recognize your new direction.

At night the danger is heightened because distances are hard to determine. Therefore, a keen lookout is required and actions must be taken early. Determine who is the stand-on (right of way) vessel and make any course changes you perform obvious and unambiguous. Hail on VHF, hail aloud, use a sound device whatever it takes to ensure you are avoiding collision. Two short blasts mean passing starboard to starboard sides. One short blast means passing port to port sides.

A good rule of thumb to use once you spot a light is to first ascertain which side of the other vessel you see via the color of the light. Then watch the bearing of that light relative to your vessel. If the bearing is unchanging, then you are likely on a collision course.

Sailboats using engine power automatically become a powerboat and must display power boat lights as below. During the day a sailboat under power greater than 12 meters must display a black cone.

Other Vessels

Where required, the "By Day" shapes are shown in the white circles.

Power Vessels (less than 50m):

One all around white plus red and green.

Large Power Ships over 50 m

Same for Power Vessels except for the addition of a forward facing mast light. In addition, in general, for all power boats below, any time you go over 50m in length you need to add another forward facing mast light.

What you have to be cognizant of is being able to imagine what this looks like at night.

For example, the container ship bearing down on you in pitch dark with look like this below. We certain hope that you never see this.

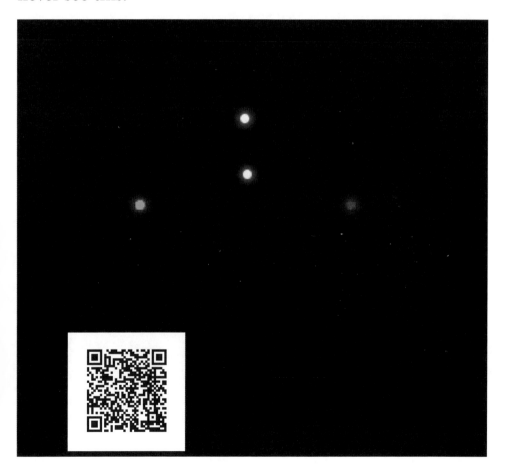

Pilot Boats - All around white over red.

Towing -Two forward facing white lights plus yellow aft.

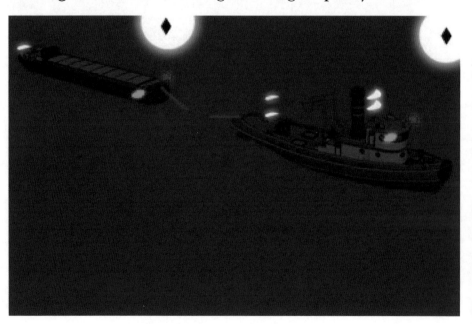

Dredging or cable laying - underwater operations -All around red over white over red. Plus two red on the danger side, two green on the non-danger side.

Fishing with a long line -Commercial fishing operation with a line. Red over white.

Fishing with nets etc - trawling - Commercial fishing operation with a nets. Green over white.

Constrained by Draft - Three Red.

Restricted in Ability to Maneuver -

Red over white over red.

Module 20: Sounds

Sound signals are defined and prescribed in the Navigation Rules for International and Inland Waters. Sound has an advantage over light signals, in that it can be used when vision fails. The use of bells, whistles, gongs, and horns etc. can be valuable in many visually impaired conditions. However, the ideal horn is one that is pressurized and can be heard for a long distance. You may want to carry a couple of these as spares.

The Navigation Rules for International sound signals vary slightly from Inland Rules. Refer to the official document for proper use in your sailing area.

The purposes of sounding devices are many including: alerting an oncoming vessel of your intentions, signaling an emergency and identifying yourself in foggy and unclear visually conditions.

These audio devices should be located so they are readily available when needed. When using sound signals there are rules governing the sounding length of time and frequency (how often you send a signal).

The basic sound signals you should know are shown below.

Visit the page where all the sounds are listed and you can hear them.

SHORT: A short blast is to be one second long

PROLONGED: A prolonged blast is to be between 4 and 6 seconds.

Between each successive signal you should wait 10 seconds or more.

These sounds are to made by power-driven vessels greater than 12 meters (39ft) in length and when operating in a narrow channel and have sighted each other.

SHORT: I am altering my course to starboard

SHORT - SHORT: I am altering my course to port

SHORT - SHORT - SHORT: I am running astern propulsion

5 RAPID BLASTS: Danger

The danger signal is general and can be used by anyone to signal disagreement with another vessel's signal, which may lead to danger or just danger in general to anyone.

Sailboat in Fog

When operating in areas of restricted visibility IE fog, a Sailboat must make the following signal.

PROLONGED - SHORT - SHORT: I am a sailboat in fog

Remember this by an average sailboat normally has two sails- thus the two shorts toots.

Powerboat in Fog

Where prolonged is a prolonged blast (lasting 4 to 6 seconds) and signals are not more than 2 minutes apart. This signal above (one prolonged and two short) is also the signal for other vessels operating in fog such as vessels towing, broken down, commercial fishing, or restricted in ability to maneuver.

Power driven vessels operating in fog must make the following signal not more than 2 minutes apart.

PROLONGED: I am a power driven vessel in fog making way

PROLONGED - PROLONGED: I am a power driven vessel in fog stopped and making no way

These are international rules. The above list of signals is not exhaustive. For a list of all sound signals visit Rules 32 through 37 of the USCG regs (which again are international).

Finally, a piece of advice: Make sure you have a loud sound making device at hand at all times near the helm available within 1-2 seconds. The day you will need it is the day you will thank yourself for heeding this advice.

Oh and BTW, that day WILL come.

Visit the page where all the sounds are listed and you can hear them.

Module 21: What Do I Do Next?

Final word by Grant Headifen - Director of Education, NauticEd.

Well done! You made it all the way through. (Unless you cheated and jumped to the end).

I bet you wish that everyone on the water would do this course. Why? Well for one, you don't want to be the only poor sod who is sailing when there are others out there who don't know this stuff - right? Well, there are a few things you can do to help.

(1) Do a facebook post "I just completed the NauticEd Navigation Rules Course App. I recommend all boaters to do this course. Search for NauticEd on the Apple App Store".

(2) How about post a sticky note on the yacht club notice board.

(3) Email a link to the course to your buds

(4) In any case, thanks for what ever you can do to spread the word of safety on the water.

There is a test associated with this course and it is online. You can see how you retained the material. The test is free. And if you liked this course we've got another free course you might like which is Basic SailTrim. If you already have a NauticEd account, the course is now in your curriculum and the test is waiting for you.

Sign-in here -->

Once you get past these few courses we think that you're ready for the big leagues - that is to start building your sailing resume.

Your sailing resume consists of theory courses you have passed, on the water sailing experience, professional instruction, behavioral training badges and the coup-de-grace - the International Certificate of Competence aka the ICC.

You see, yacht charter companies require a resume every time they charter out a yacht. They will not accept a stand alone sailing certification, they want to see all your experience theory and practical. And yacht charter companies accept the NauticEd Resume. View this video -->

So with that, we have another free gift for you, the NauticEd online sailing logbook. There you can store all of your sailing and boating outings. The algorithm that we have developed matches up your experience with your theory courses and issues you a rank. That rank along with the summary presented logbook you can take to the insurance companies and the yacht charter companies.

We invite you to do the following:

(1) Set up a free account at NauticEd

(2) Take the free Navigation Rules course test which is waiting for you free in your curriculum

(3) Enter your previous sailing experience into our free cloud based logbook

(4) We have also developed a free course calculator that works personally and specifically for you. You answer a few questions about your sailing habits and the calculator determines which courses you should take.

Go here for the calculator -->

(5) Start building your sailing resume via our courses and your logged experience.

(6) Finally, we recommend that you go for the gusto and achieve for yourself the International Certificate of Competence, the ICC. Especially if you plan on sailing in Europe, you will be required by Yacht Charter companies and local governments to have this. To gain the ICC, you will need to pass both the theory and practical portions of the RYA Day Skipper Course.

Visit our RYA Day Skipper Course here

There is so much more to NauticEd than just a few free courses and I invite you to check us out fully. If you're into sailing, I guarantee you'll be into us.

Visit here for other NauticEd Sailing Courses you might like:

Here is a List of Excellent Courses

- Skipper

- RYA Day Skipper (for ICC purposes)

- Bareboat Charter

- Anchoring

- Maneuvering Under Power

- Coastal Navigation

- Catamaran Sailing Confidence

- BVI Chart Briefing
- Electronic Navigation
- Basic Sail Trim
- Storm Tactics
- Weather
- Safety at Sea
- Sail Trim
- Introductory Celestial Navigation
- Your First Weekend in Dinghy Sailing

And here is a great kids eBook you might like: Alex Learns to Sail

I hope to see you on the water somewhere. I'll recognize you because you'll be the one obeying the International Rules of Prevention of Collision at Sea. :)

Sincerely,

Grant Headifen

Director of Education - NauticEd

Made in the USA
Lexington, KY
02 July 2016